How to Live with a Neurotic Dog

Stephen Baker

with Illustrations by Fred Hilliard

D0754327

Virgin

The masculine pronoun *he* is used throughout the book for
grammatical simplicity only. No sexism intended. This author
believes firmly in equality between sexes, be that among dog
owners or their dogs.

This edition first published in Great Britain in 1993 by
Virgin Books
an imprint of Virgin Publishing Ltd
332 Ladbroke Grove
London W10 5AH

Reprinted 1993

First published in Great Britain in 1989 by
W. H. Allen & Co. Plc

ISBN 0 86369 730 5

Printed and bound in Great Britain by
Cox & Wyman Ltd, Reading, Berkshire

Stephen Baker is the author of 21 books, about equally divided between humour bestsellers such as *How to Live with a Neurotic Cat* and professional works in the field of advertising and marketing. Twice nominated as Art Director of the Year, he is now president of his own advertising and marketing firm in New York City.

Fred Hilliard was born and raised in the kind of small western towns where knowing your dog in a close-up and personal way was normal – a background invaluable in creating the illustrations for this book. Even more invaluable has been the advice and encouragement of Buck, the Hilliards' family dog and Fred's trusted confidant. Fred, his wife, two children and Buck live on an island about ten miles off the coast in Puget Sound.

To Murray,
a dog of uncertain origin,
without whose help this book
would have been finished
a long time ago

Contents

1
What Makes a Dog Neurotic?   1

2
Training the Neurotic Dog   16

3
Sleeping Habits of the Neurotic Dog   36

4
How to Dress and Groom the Neurotic Dog   50

5
Traveling with the Neurotic Dog   64

6
Feeding the Neurotic Dog   78

7
The Neurotic Dog vs. Baby   88

8
The Neurotic Dog and Your Cat   100

9
How to Play with a Neurotic Dog   110

10
Analyzing the Neurotic Dog at Home   120

11
Can the Neurotic Dog Be Cured?   136

CHAPTER 1

What Makes a Dog Neurotic?

We must, first of all, try to understand the neurotic dog. Our understanding of him is the key to his happiness, if not ours.

There is a reason for everything a dog does. In his opinion, these reasons are valid, whether we, the owners, think so or not. If, for example, he is the first to reach the food on the dining room table, there is a reason for his getting there before anyone else. He's hungry.

A great many dogs are neurotic, especially in the English-speaking countries. Today, the canine population is about 100 million. Out of this, about 100 million can be classified as neurotic – a conservative estimate.

It is common knowledge among psychiatrists by now that neurosis among dogs is on the rise. More and more dog owners are seeking psychiatric treatment for their pets.

Today's dog lives under more pressure than ever before. His is a busy schedule. Chores confront him every minute during waking hours, straining his physical stamina—not to mention his intellect—to the limit.

1

Here is what an average dog has to put up with in the course of a typical day:

7:30–7:55 A.M.	Thinks about getting up.
7:55–8:00 A.M.	Jumps off bed and does stretching exercises. Goes to kitchen to find out what's available in way of food.
8:00–10:00 A.M.	Returns to the bedroom to continue his sleep on a fuller stomach.
10:00–11:30 A.M.	Goes to the window to check traffic outside.
11:30–12:00 A.M.	Before-meal siesta in bedroom.
12:00–12:45 P.M.	Adjourns to living room sofa to take advantage of sun spot there.
12:45–1:30 P.M.	Pushed off sofa. Returns to bedroom in search of privacy.
1:30–3:00 P.M.	Asked to leave the bedroom and chased off the sofa again, dog finds solace on the second bookshelf in the living room. Long nap.

3:00–3:10 P.M.	Greets children returning from school. Jumps up and down, wags tail, licks faces, pretending he is happy to see them.
3:10–3:51 P.M.	Examines his dish in the kitchen and sniffs at his food. Makes a face.
3:51–4:15 P.M.	Joins group at dining table.
4:15–5:30 P.M.	After-meal siesta.
5:30–6:30 P.M.	Leaves house to call next door. Gets into an argument with the dog living there.
6:30–7:00 P.M.	Tired and disheveled, his coat covered with mixture of dry blood and mud, dog shows up at home.
7:00–7:30 P.M.	He is picked up and summarily put in the bathtub for thorough soaking, adding insult to injury.
7:00–7:35 P.M.	Dried off with large towel, but escapes before ordeal is finished.
7:35–8:00 P.M.	Leaves home, visits dog next door again to resolve argument. This time, he wins.
8:00–8:30 P.M.	Appears in the kitchen promptly to help with preparation of dinner.
8:30–9:15 P.M.	Joins family at the dinner table. Retires to living room to watch television. Bored by the program, he dozes off.
9:15–9:16 P.M.	Opens up both eyes and leaves for the bedroom.
9:16–9:20 P.M.	Unmakes bed.
9:20 P.M.	Dog-tired, he goes to sleep for the night. Tomorrow: another dog's day.

When he enters the world, a dog has few, if any, emotional problems. Not yet having to face reality, he is optimistic about his future. As with a human infant, it is only later in life that problems occur—say, a minute or two after birth.

One of the thoughts which comes to the mind of the newly arrived dog and which strikes him as a brilliant notion is *eating*. It is then that he first discovers the fiercely competitive nature of his environment. Instinct pushes him toward satisfying his hunger, but now he finds obstacles in his way, such as his small but equally determined brothers and sisters, all heading in the same direction.

The older the dog, the more he realizes what he is up against. Everywhere he looks, he sees other dogs much like him; they can be bought for a price. Shocking indeed is the discovery that he can be replaced.

GENERIC
DOGS
Get One Free!

Reminding the dog of his inadequacy are the past and present heroes whose accomplishments dwarf his. A watchdog called Cerberus, for example, made a name for himself guarding the gates of Hades, though not too well in spite of his no fewer than three heads—quite unusual for a dog. He was followed by such renowned figures as Rin-Tin-Tin, Lassie, Snoopy, MacKenzie, Superdog, and many others. In such company, who would not have his ego bruised?

 =

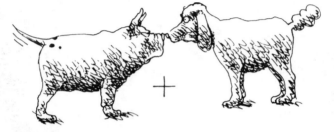 =

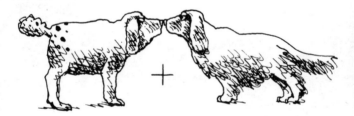 =

 =

Dogs of mixed heritage are often made to feel socially inferior. Untainted line of descent allows dog to show off his talents at dog shows, while doors are shut to the most numerous and by far the most successful breed of all: the mutt.

Bigger, if not better, than dog
is the owner.

Our culture makes severe demands on the dog. We humans accept, mostly on hearsay, the premise that "dog is man's best friend" and let it go at that. For the dog, this is a debatable issue. He knows that, if anything, the reverse holds true. It is man who is dog's best friend.

Unless the dog grows up to be a Saint Bernard or a Great Dane, which not all dogs are able to do, he will be at the mercy of his master. A two-legged stance enables man to look *down* at his pet, disdainfully if so inclined. This vantage point gives the owner a pervading sense of superiority, a state of mind that makes him a difficult, if not impossible, person to live with.

Even to a young dog it soon becomes obvious that his chief problem in life is, and always will be, his master. Because he uses only his legs to walk, man has his hands free to do other things. For example, he can grasp the dog by the scruff of his neck to deposit him elsewhere, inside or outside the home, several miles away perhaps.

A dog's instinct, let alone common sense, tells him that feeding time is all day. However, in typically human fashion, dog owners cling to the notion that their pets should be on some kind of feeding schedule. Man insists on giving a dog only one or two meals a day instead of a hundred.

Dog's natural habitat is on top of a bed, preferably freshly made. His sense of self-preservation tells him this is where he belongs. Many owners, ignorant of the physical and emotional needs of their dog, keep interrupting their pet's daily twenty-four-hour nap and insist that he rest on the floor, which, as even people know, is not nearly as soft as a bed.

It is just for such reasons that dog learns early in life to depend in his intellect rather than his size. He realistically

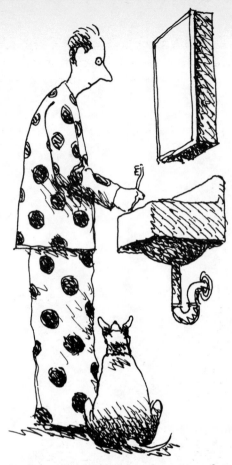

accepts the fact that nature made man a larger, more
ponderous creature who uses his sheer weight to make his
points, however absurd these might be. But dog knows that
physical prowess puts his master at only a temporary advantage, and in the long run dog's superior reasoning
power will win out. And so, quietly but with remarkable
efficiency, dog fights his battle against man. In the process
he often becomes neurotic. So does his owner.

Is It Any Wonder
Dogs Get Neurotic?

Summary

1. **DO** be patient with your neurotic dog. Try to understand the underlying cause of his neurosis. It's you.

2. **DON'T** praise other dogs in his presence. Consider his feelings.

3. **DO** take into account his basic psychological needs, such as food, shelter, and a color television set in the living room.

4. **DON'T** make your mutt feel unwanted. Tell him that ours is a proud nation of many different descents.

5. **DO** remember: dog's best friend is man, not the other way around.

CHAPTER 2

Training the Neurotic Dog

It isn't too difficult to train a neurotic dog, provided you use psychology instead of common sense.

His education should start at an early age. It may take the dog a lifetime to learn. "You can't teach an old dog new tricks" is only true in part. You can't teach new tricks to a young dog either.

This does not mean that his is a simple mind. More often than not, the failure of communication between owner and dog is due to the language barrier between them. The dog simply does not know what his master is trying to tell him. This should hardly be surprising. Few people achieve proficiency in barking; when they try, their pitiful attempts only tend to confuse the dog.

It has yet to be proven to a dog that his readiness to obey will serve his best interest. Cats hardly ever pay attention to a command, yet they have long since gained man's respect. Other pets, such as fish and gremlins, pay even less attention. Yet they get fed as often as the dog does.

Nevertheless, dogs have been known to comply with

their masters' wishes, or at least pretend to go through the motions. Their decision to obey is usually based on practical, not philosophical, considerations. They have learned a long time ago from advice passed down from generation to generation that a show of affection is the quickest way to get what you want; which is why they secretly practice the art in front of the mirror every morning.

Fundamentally, teaching a dog means developing his ability to free-associate; that is, to connect your words with anything that may prove useful to him. As discovered through laboratory experiments conducted by Ivan P. Pavlov, and since confirmed by everyone who ever owned a dog, it is possible to teach the species to react by instinct to the same sounds and gestures, if repeated often enough and loud enough. The words *dinner on the table*, for example, are capable of arousing a dog from the deepest of comatose states. Remarkably, his knee-jerk reflexes will propel his body (often with his eyes still tightly shut) in the general direction of the kitchen.

Ability to form
mental pictures in
advance improves
dog's ability to
respond to stimuli
and act quickly.
This is important
for his survival.

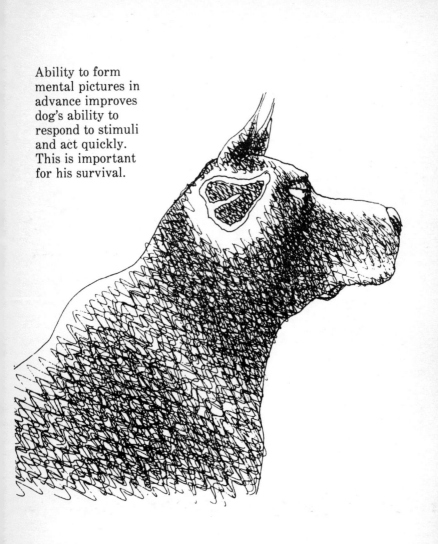

Dogs, like human infants, learn by imitation. *Show* him what you want; whether or not he performs, he will be duly amused by your hilarious attempts to please him.

EVERY ENGLISH-SPEAKING DOG SHOULD AT LEAST UNDERSTAND THE BASIC COMMANDS "NO," "SIT," "HEEL," "DOWN," "COME HERE," AND "HEY, NOT ON THE CARPET." USE OF FOUL LANGUAGE IS LEFT UP TO THE OWNER'S DISCRETION, VOCABULARY, AND LUNG CAPACITY. ON THE FOLLOWING PAGES ARE HELPFUL SUGGESTIONS FOR GETTING YOUR DOG'S ATTENTION AND KEEPING IT—FOR A MOMENT OR TWO.

NO — O — O — OO — O

THE "NO" COMMAND

One of the most important words in your dog's vocabulary is "no". He must learn that the term is the antonym of "yes", even though they sound so similar to him as to often cause confusion.

The word "no" should be used only if absolutely necessary and then with care and compassion. A sharp "no" may offend the dog and cause him to sulk. One of the ways to soften your "no" is to deliver it in a series, as in, "No, no, NO." The emphasis is on the last "no." A modification of the basic "No, no, NO" is "No, no, no, NO." Repetition is especially effective with a weary animal; four no's will keep him awake longer than three.

An excellent version of the short peremptory "no" command is one especially popular with women dog fanciers, more accustomed to using gentle persuasion. It goes something like this: "No-o-o. No-o-o. Sha-a-a-me on you." The first "no" starts at a low note, then works gradually to a higher pitch until the voice cracks and gives out completely. The same command can also be delivered the other way around, starting at a high pitch. Should your dog be musically inclined, both versions will please him; they remind him of his mother pleading with him.

Dog owners with a pendantic bent will even try spelling out the word, as in "No! You understand? N-O." This often proves to be an exercise in futility. Even those with a modicum of education know how to spell a two-letter word. The implication that your listener does not is an insult to his intelligence.

21

MAKING YOUR DOG SIT

Every dog should know how to sit. He should not lie on the floor sleeping all of the time.

The first problem to overcome in teaching your neurotic dog to *sit down* is making him *get up*. Touch him gently on the back. If this fails to awaken him, touch again, this time with more authority. If he still does not respond (as he probably won't), lift him slowly by the nape of his neck, or ears if they are long enough.

Once you have succeeded in making your dog sit, try persuading him to stay that way, first for one or two seconds, and then for three, four, or even five. Admittedly, this is the hard part, since dog's natural inclination is to return to his original prone position at the soonest possible moment. Don't give up; if you don't succeed the first time, try again. Well-trained dogs have been known to stay sitting up for as long as half a minute. Praise your dog profusely for his excellent performance even if he gets anywhere near to that.

Step One

Step Two

Step Three

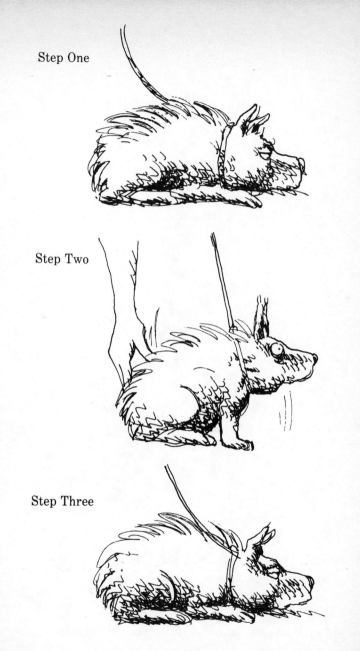

TRAINING THE DOG TO HEEL

There are times in every dog's life when
he must be taken for a walk, especially when
his home is an apartment several stories above
street level and tossing him out the window becomes a

24

less than satisfactory solution—to the dog, at least.

Taking a pet for a walk requires a leash and collar. The idea is that these implements will dissuade the dog from carrying out his natural desire to go his, not your, way.

Authorities on dog training agree that consistency is important. Your instructions must be clear not only to you, but also to your dog. It is best that your pet learn to stay near your left knee and does not change sides for his own amusement. Never permit your dog to walk on your right side. It is up to you to *always* keep to *his* right. You can speed up the learning process by staying close to him. If you feel your dog wants to look around, look around with him. If he wants to cross the street, then cross the street. Make sure that you come to a full stop at every fire hydrant, tree, or other dog.

At times you may find that the leash has tied up your legs so that neither of you can walk freely. Do not despair. If you become so hopelessly entangled that you can no longer move, ask someone to help unwind you.

TEACHING THE "DOWN" COMMAND

Not much effort is needed to make the neurotic dog fully understand and approve—heartily—the command *down*. As pointed out earlier, the chief problem is teaching him the meaning of the command *up*.

TRAINING YOUR DOG TO COME

To teach your dog to come you will need the collar again, a cord about fifty feet long, and the dog himself.

Attach one end of the cord to the collar and hold on firmly to the other end. Allow the dog to follow his instinct and walk about ten or fifteen feet away from you. If he refuses to cover such a long distance, *you* walk away. Then say as if you mean business, "Come here."

If there is no reaction, try, "Please come here," or, perhaps, "Will you be good enough to come here, please?" If your plea still falls on deaf ears, gently draw back the line. If still nothing happens, keep tugging, this time with more authority. Then once more, using all your might, pull at the cord and scream at the top of your voice. Now get up from the ground and replace the broken cord.

Weeks of concentrated training in pulling the dog toward you while he remains fixed in his original down position will bring surprising results. You will note sub-

stantial gains in your muscular development, particularly in the area of the back, shoulders, and kneecaps. Yelling at him will help your aerobic capacity. What's more, you will probably lose some weight, if not the dog.

HOUSEBREAKING

A dog who is not housebroken can be a source of embarrassment to his owner, especially if he has visitors who are not well-disposed toward the canine species and have an acute sense of smell. For this reason if no other, most dog owners insist that their pets learn to distinguish between table legs and fire hydrants, even if they may appear to be the same to the dog.

The toilet training received in early life by the neurotic dog is extremely significant from a psychological point of view. Confused concepts later result in serious emotional disturbances for the owner.

You should be neither too lenient nor too harsh with your growing puppy. Overindulgence on your part may lead him to think of your living room as one giant bathroom. Overly stern discipline, on the other hand, may intimidate him to such a degree that he will refuse to heed the call of nature *anywhere* under *any* circumstances for the rest of his life.

Training your dog to use the outdoors is really not as complicated as it seems. Training should begin with a

constant vigil lasting for four or five days. It is best to start the lessons at the beginning of a two weeks' vacation so that you will be able to fully concentrate on the task at hand. Drink a lot of coffee and keep all the house lights on at night, so you can keep your eyes on your dog at all times.

Close supervision will enable you to catch him in the act. React by crying "No!" at the top of your voice. Then explain: "You made a mistake!" Depending on your dog's attention span, you may go into further details. After a week or so, catch up on your sleep.

Those sharing an apartment with their dog often find the so-called newspaper technique to be the most practical method of all. Spread several pages on the floor. For small dogs, three to five pages will do; for medium-sized dogs, seven to ten; for large breeds, use the entire edition of the Sunday *New York Times*.

It should be remembered that the average canine has the same dislike of slovenly homes as the human. His preference for clean living quarters shows itself in his insistence on returning to the same spot over and over again.

Administration was "a minimum condition of iscal health."

ather amazing to contemplate the fact e was only one other occasion prior to of this year when a substantial budget vas even planned. That was in the case udget for fiscal 1949 when President proposed a $4.8 billion surplus designed at inflation. But actual expenditures billion higher than had been estimated, ceipts fell short of estimates by $4.3 he result being a $1.8 billion deficit.

Anti-Welfare Drive

e concerned about the state of mind le New York Legislature on the subject welfare support for the needy. Hardly ases that dispatches from Albany do t some new evidence of antagonism to elfare, or a blind determination to cut o the taxpayer, or a new effort to sur- e state with a wall that will scare away eking new job opportunity, or to "get ith families on relief. An unreasoning s to "do something" about relief seems de the Albany scene, and even, when ive is good, as to assure vigilance raud and malingering on welfare rolls, vise methods emerge.

after passage in both Senate and Assem bill has gone to Governor Rockefeller ld permit local welfare departments case workers and investigators w ho had not even graduated from lone had any social-work experi n appalling thought that a out of high school should o deal with the complex p e arisen, for instance, bandoned a wife and at recent high school amily. A welfare w tuation, just to do th lling what the fami lars. He or she i human problem ome self-suppo ortant job in 16 of wise, exper ng enough to college gradu subject and ha e confident th bill comes fro a shortage of e lower the stan welfare, put it we can only se of social welf d in prudent the needy th fork should b re standards on and under We hope to the Legislat

od Man Retires

ws that Charles Gilman will retire Administrator of Business Affairs for d of Education evokes mixed feelings v, we wish him well. His fifty-two years ary service with the school system—he rose from office boy to the board's ess officer—entitle him to every second the same time there is a certain sad he thought that Mr. Gilman, a man of rmth and wit, is leaving active service. itizens Budget Commission declared in en they awarded him a gold medal for rvice to the city," Mr. Gilman has

---

sands cross in their daily travels of the long range missile and to cut Throughout its history this island of to a minimum Russia's surface navy Manhattan has been the scene of He is studying the possibilities of one episode after another in the long switching his entire army over to a progress toward that ideal state of territorial system subject only to human society toward which men intermittent call-ups. continue to grope. Today this same island is the seat of an international wholly surprising. For imitation is body dedicated to the guidance and the sincerest form of flattery. And enlightenment of that groping Khrushchev is adopting many NATO search, and on this particular day, methods. the status of a crown colony and the responsibilities of its own under the the Kremlin created its "anti-able direction of the first native of NATO" Warsaw alliance with at Ireland ever to rule here. least 'the pretense of a similar or-

When the Duke of York ascended the British throne as James II Feb. 6, 1685. Had been a under his patronage

This strategic revolution is not

After NATO was first established,

---

which has now materialized in the International Development Associa-tion, formed as an affiliate of the World Bank. The purpose of the I. D. A. is to make additional fi-nancing facilities available to the under-developed nations, mainly through the making of "soft" loans.

Without wishing in any way to minimize the importance of Senator Monroney's contribution to this project, it is only fair to point out that the idea was first developed in the far-seeing report, "Partner-ship Progress," made to President Tru-man in March, 1951, by the Interna-tional Development Advisory Board under the chairmanship of Nelson A. Rockefeller.

Some dogs just don't want to learn. It is a matter of principle with them; they find it difficult to accept their master as a source of authority—or a source of any type of information, for that matter.

Should that be the case, you may want to turn to a professional trainer to pick up where you left off. In most cities there are experts familiar with the subtleties of canine persuasion and the value of a summary kick in the behind. Many have come from wild animal training backgrounds; lion tamers are especially popular.

At first, your dog may be reluctant to enter school, finding the whole idea repugnant and much beneath his dignity. Try convincing your dog first by having a long and serious talk with him.

Should he resist, try using gentle persuasion.

As time goes on, your dog may yet become an exemplary student. Dog trainers know how to get through to

their students. The day soon arrives . . . when your dog finally graduates. What a source of pride it is to have a well-educated dog in the house now, someone who not only knows more than dogs without a degree, but who is also so intellectually superior as to put you and your friends to shame.

Summary

1. **DO** make sure your dog understands what you mean. Use proper grammar and enunciate your words clearly. Dogs disdain sloppy language.

2. **DON'T** try to communicate with your dog in his own language for purposes of saving time. Barking does not come easily to people.

3. **DO** discuss problems with your dog. Dogs prefer persuasion to force. If you see him yawn, stop.

4. **DON'T** forget: you cannot live with a dog who is not housebroken. You must move out.

5. **DO** show your dog what it is you want him to do: jump, roll over, fetch a ball. Dogs learn more by first-hand observation than from textbooks.

CHAPTER 3

Sleeping Habits of the Neurotic Dog

A dog needs sleep to rebound, to gain enough energy to go from the bedroom to the kitchen, stop at the living room couch, and accompany his master outdoors when forced to so do. It is no wonder then that he will require a minimum of twenty-four hours of rest a day, or more.

Occasionally one hears of owners keeping their dogs awake for several consecutive hours. Your pet should not be asked to go to such extremes. Sooner or later, prolonged interruptions between naps will lead to serious depression, not to mention the effect they will have on his already shaky opinion of you and all that you stand for.

Those who truly care about the well-being of their pet will take into account his everyday physical comfort. Admittedly, this may be more easily said than done. In today's homes, much of the furniture is designed for those who control the checkbook, not those who use it more frequently than anyone else.

Side chairs are built to provide support to the lower part of the human anatomy, but fail to accommodate size and shape of the canine body.

Beanbags fail to take into account dog's natural tendency to lie on his belly, not his back.

Coffee-table tops are much too hard for a dog trying to find a place to relax.

The accommodation that seems to best answer dog's never-ending search for suitable sleeping quarters is the bed.

Dogs rank the bed among man's most ingenious inventions, a testimony to his capacity to come up with a useful item at long last, and this in the face of his serious intellectual limitations. In the canine world, the bed is put on par with the innerspring mattress and the garbage can in terms of both beauty and practicality.

Not even the living room couch can compete with this piece of furniture. The top of the bed allows the dog to stretch out in any direction he wishes. He can shift his position freely; in the daytime he can find the sunniest spot, at night the softest. If the temperature falls below the required comfort level, he can simply pull the bedspread off the bed and climb under the blanket. The sheets are reasonably clean, in contrast with carpets and other floor coverings that come in direct contact with the soles of shoes and, worse still, man's stocking feet. Available too are pillows, light enough to carry from one side of the bed to another.

What's more, dog is able to find privacy in the bedroom through most of the day; he can sleep undisturbed. In the kitchen he may be stepped on, or he may step on someone's feet; in the living room he may inadvertently—or advertently—be sat on, while reclining on the couch. But in the bedroom he has the opportunity to get away from the rest of the household, his true motives beyond suspicion.

The bed has only one disadvantage, and that is that this area may have to be shared with someone else. Dogs often find their midday siesta rudely interrupted at eleven or so at night for that reason. Negotiations for territorial rights then begin. Disputes are usually settled on the basis of available space and size of teeth of the respective parties.

No dog likes to share his bed with another person, but given no choice he will try his best to cope. Some people consider a dog a strange bedfellow; all dogs consider people that.

The sleepwalker prefers to take shortcuts to get where he wants to go.

The member of the family wants to share every minute with those he loves. He is even willing to let a third party move into his space.

The jumper can hardly wait to go to bed. The mattress is soft enough to absorb his landing. So is the owner's stomach.

The early riser wakes with the sun and welcomes the day with a burst of enthusiasm. He likes to share his feelings with others. Having done so, he promptly goes back to sleep.

The faithful companion happily joins his master in the kitchen. Having gone for several hours without food, he is perishing with hunger. He will have his snack at the kitchen table, on his way back, or in bed.

The burrower knows that it is warmer *under* the blanket.
Experience taught him how to get there fast—using the
back-door approach. Should there be less than enough
room for both occupants, this situation can easily be
rectified (see below).

The large dog would not mind sharing the bed with
another person but, unfortunately, there is only room for
one.

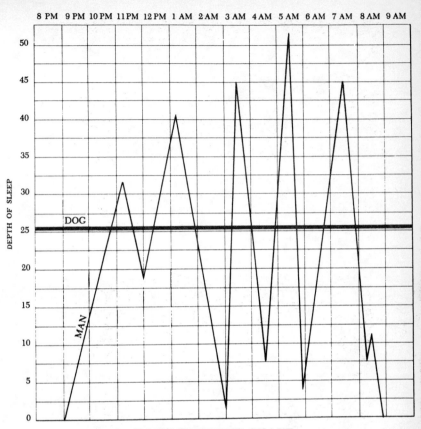

DOG'S SLEEPING CHART

As far as dog is concerned, people have curious sleeping habits. They are anything but calm. Kicking and arm wrestling through the night, they wake up in the morning as if they had never gone to sleep in the first place. During the night they mumble words even more incomprehensible than those they utter during daytime. In sharp contrast to such nocturnal exercises is the dog's sleeping pattern.

45

46

Some dog owners would just as soon have the bed all for themselves. The problem they face is how to persuade the dog to give up the space which he feels belongs to him, if not legally, then morally.

These steps serve as a general guide:

First, find the dog. A bump under the blanket will clearly indicate his presence. Push down on him to let him know you are there. Chances are good he will make an appearance at one end of the blanket to ask you to kindly get lost.

Now lift up the blanket gently, unpeeling it from his body, as it were. He will get the message and bare his teeth. Do not be intimidated by this show of force; it is a ploy. Do not take his snarling seriously either; it is a throwback to his ancestry and comes as naturally to him as cursing does to you. Stand your ground; show him who is the boss.

He will then try taking your hand in his mouth. No problem. Simply tear off part of the sheet for bandages, and use it as a tourniquet until the ambulance arrives.

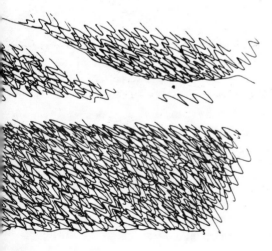

A well-known method of keeping dogs off their masters' beds (approved by the Society for the Prevention of Cruelty to Animals and also by dogs themselves) is to build a bed for canine use only.

To make sleeping quarters more inviting to a dog, it must have features all of its own. A fire hydrant (1) gives reason to get out of bed for a short walk. Tree trunk (2) offers an acceptable alternative, not to mention a change of pace. Inner tube with moving floor belt (3) allows dog to give chase to an object without having to go outdoors, while garbage can (4) filled to the brim with leftover goodies makes the trip all the more worthwhile.

Summary

1. **DO** remember a dog needs sleep when he is tired, which is at all times. As said before, his is not an easy existence; he lives a dog's life.

2. **DON'T** disturb him while he is getting his well-deserved rest. Speak only in a whisper and walk on tip-toe. Have an alarm system installed in your home. Burglars are notoriously inconsiderate.

3. **DO** get a soft, comfortable bed. Your dog will appreciate your thoughtfulness.

4. **DON'T** let him interfere with your sleeping schedule. If he wakes you up often, go sleep on the living room sofa.

5. **DO** try an electric blanket for cold nights. Dogs like warmth.

6. **DON'T** ever, ever snore. Dogs dislike the sound; it reminds them of other dogs who are bigger than they are.

CHAPTER 4

How to Dress and Groom the Neurotic Dog

For centuries dogs ran around naked. Civilization put an end to that. There are more well-dressed dogs on the streets today than there are well-dressed people.

It is important that your pet keeps up with the dictates of fashion. Nothing is more embarrassing to a dog than appearing in public in last year's outfits. As the saying goes, "Clothes make the dog." A poorly coordinated wardrobe suggests questionable taste, not to mention class. It's not that a dog particularly cares what people think of him; he is more concerned about the impression he makes on his peers he meets outside the home. Remember, dogs dress for each other. Nothing can be more upsetting to them than going out and having *nothing to wear*.

There are also practical reasons for his being properly arrayed in the outdoors. He will be less exposed to the elements, including the splash of passing cars and that of other dogs. Then, too, clothing keeps the dog relatively

clean. Washing his clothes is less trouble than washing him; few owners would throw their dogs into a washing machine and take a chance of clogging up the appliance.

What's more, clothes often help the dog tell the difference between male or female, even at a distance. Thus, he may be spared the trouble of having to stop and check, only to find that he could have better spent his time on meeting someone else.

Dogs may not admit it, but nothing less than their self-image may be at stake as they pass a better-dressed dog on the street. The average dog knows full well that without his clothes on he may look just like any other dog.

Clothes should fit not only the dog but the occasion. Fortunately, today's owner is able to select from a variety of styles designed to improve his dog's appearance.

The jogger's outfit is for your dog doing his daily constitutional.

In the summer you may decide to allow your dog to walk around barely covered. A well-chosen hat could be all he needs to appear fully dressed.

In the winter you may find that another layer of fur not only will keep your dog warm but will also make him look better than when wearing only his own.

53

For dogs resentful of having to wear the same outfit again and again, consider the purchase of one or more hats. They do wonders for a dog's profile; he is sure to be the envy of his canine friends up and down the street.

The hunting cap lends dog a stern, even menacing look, useful when encountering other members of his species larger than he is. A perennial favorite with hounds, retrievers, and pointers.

The fedora gives dog a more imposing formal demeanor. *De rigueur* at weddings, funerals, and corporate boardroom meetings.

The ten-gallon hat suggests ownership of livestock and oil wells. Wide brim protects wearer from pigeon droppings.

The knitted cap can be worn folded up or down, depending on weather conditions. Some dogs like to cover their ears with it to cut down on outside noise, such as your voice.

54

Female dogs think bathing suits become them. They may not go into the water, but they know that on dry land they are bound to make an impression on the opposite sex.

Male dogs prefer the sporty look for resort wear, a simple combination of briefs and shirt that connotes a casual, moneyed lifestyle.

And then there are the skinny-dippers.

Most dog owners are under the impression that dogs don't like baths. The reason they think this is that dogs hate baths.

However, we must try to understand the psychological basis for dogs' aversion to soap and water. Common sense tells dog that actually there is no need for him to get into a tub. He may smell bad to his owners, but this is a matter of opinion. To other dogs he smells just the way he should. In fact, a washed dog is often ostracized by his canine friends until he becomes his old self again.

Here is how you can survive giving your dog a bath.

First, tell your dog that cleanliness is next to godliness while carrying him to his bath.

Place him in the tub. Use force if he resists. If you slip and fall into the water, get out and continue as if nothing had happened.

Scrub him thoroughly, sparing no effort. Use a towel if you get wet. Keep talking to him in a low, soothing voice—perhaps even sing to him. Explain that soap is to cleanse, not to eat.

Refreshed by the bath, and glad that it's all over, dog will want to work off pent-up energy. Encourage him to roam around the house a bit, to be himself.

Let him shake himself.
Then wipe up the puddle
he leaves behind.

59

NOW REST.

A Well-Groomed Dog Is a Happy Dog

Summary

1. **DON'T** embarrass you dog by making him go out in the buff.

2. **DO** take you dog with you when you shop for clothes for him. Avoid discount stores. Your dog may think you are cheap.

3. **DON'T** forget to leave openings for his tail and head.

4. **DO** make sure the clothes fit. If your dog is on the plump side, consider specialty shops such as the Big Dog, the Greater Canine, and the Round Hound.

5. **DON'T** discourage your dog from admiring his image in the mirror. He has reasons to be proud.

CHAPTER 5

Traveling with the Neurotic Dog

Dogs approve of traveling. It gives them a sense of getting away from it all—their environment, their masters. They welcome the change of scenery and making contact with new people, new dogs, new beds. They can now look forward to better accommodations, better service, and most of all, better food. Resort cuisine is a vast improvement over the home-cooked kind; chefs know how to prepare food and serve it to their guests in a tasteful, professional way.

As a rule, dogs think well of the means of transportation devised by man, except, possibly for the dog-sled. It makes little if any difference to dogs whether they are taken from point A to point B by air, sea, or land, as long as they are allowed to remain in their natural prone horizontal position en route. They find the idea of covering distances with no effort on their part much to their liking—a giant step for dogdom.

64

Even traveling by car meets dog's approval, provided his needs are fulfilled. Shown here are ways of making his trip more pleasant.

Ideally suited to the emotional needs of the traveling dog is the backseat of the car, where he can stretch out.

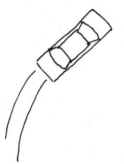

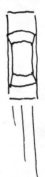

Good driving habits will permit dog to sleep uninterrupted. Turns should be made slowly, no more than five to ten miles an hour. Avoid the sound of screeching tires.

Come to a halt gradually. Sudden stops will jar the dog; even if he doesn't wake up, the jolt may cause him to have a bad dream. Keep away from stop signs. Dogs find the word "stop" annoying in any form.

Considering what they have to put up with, dogs have made remarkable adjustments to traveling on wheels. Wise owners have learned not to interfere with the dog's enjoyment of the trip; they let him be himself—a dog. Remember, it was your idea to take this trip, not his.

The sightseer keeps an eye on the passing scenery and growls at any passing car that carries a dog. For clearer visibility, he prefers traveling with the windows rolled down, summer or winter.

The lap dog demonstrates his affection by sitting in the driver's lap.

The recluse wants his privacy and will look for the
darkest corners in the car where he can think about his
problems.

The joiner shares his presence with others in the car.

The rear guard best observes the world through the back window. He can see it all without having to lift or rotate his head; rolling his eyeballs will suffice.

Dogs consider the interior of a car theirs and theirs alone, and they are prepared to protect this area against any and all intruders. Filling station attendants definitely fall under the heading of intruders. This can prove to be a problem—if not for the dog, then for the attendant and the dog owner.

Try preventing bodily contact between dog and gas station attendant throughout the transaction by keeping the windows completely or partly closed. Listed below are the three basic ways for you to maintain communication, whatever the barriers.

1. **Yell** instructions from inside the car.
2. **Use hand signals** to indicate number of gallons wanted.
3. **Roll down the window** only if you carry maximum bodily injury liability.

Safety belts are for the protection of passengers. Dog stays put when firmly fastened to the seat. Resist the use of glue; it will not hold the animal down but only raise your seat along with his body should he decide to get up.

71

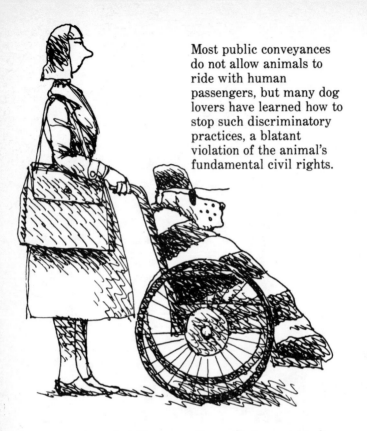

Most public conveyances do not allow animals to ride with human passengers, but many dog lovers have learned how to stop such discriminatory practices, a blatant violation of the animal's fundamental civil rights.

Railroads and airlines usually request owners to keep their beloved pets in some kind of container. They have special traveling cases for this purpose, but those specially made at home to fit your pet's needs provide added comfort. Airholes allow dog to take occasional breaths of fresh air and keep himself apprised of his surroundings.

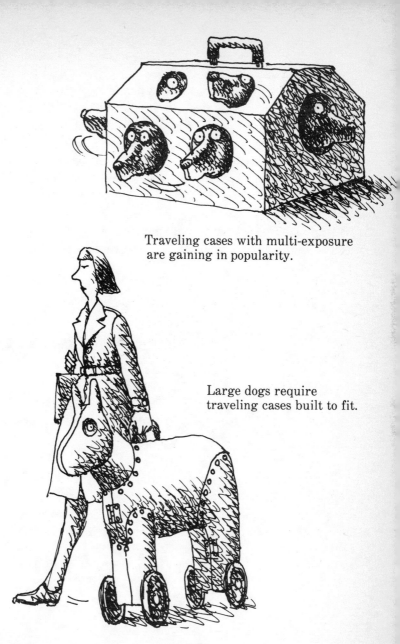

Traveling cases with multi-exposure
are gaining in popularity.

Large dogs require
traveling cases built to fit.

When planning their vacations, dog owners often ask: What kind of vacation is best for my pet? Where can he regain his peace of mind once again?

Actually, the needs of dogs are simple and basic. Food is one of them; a hotel that will serve a steak too rare or too well-done won't do, for example. Dogs especially like the custom of having breakfast served in bed. Also, dogs prefer to relax on well-made beds during the day, so the maid service might be given some thought before choosing a hotel.

Organized social activity, so much a part of many vacation routines, holds no particular interest for dogs who

know their agenda. Nature has endowed them with the ability to organize their day and never experience a dull moment. They are especially adept at scheduling their rest periods.

Perhaps the greatest dilemma dog owners face when choosing the right vacation spot is whether mountain resorts are preferable to seashore places.

As a rule, dogs prefer the seashore. Their choice is based on simple logic. Mountain terrains tend to be rugged, and not infrequently, require dog to walk uphill. In contrast, ocean beaches are flat, and they are covered with soft, absorbent sand.

On the beaches one may frequently notice dogs engaged in various digging operations. Studies show there are several deep-seated psychological reasons for their wanting to go below the surface of this planet:

1. To get away from people (escape mechanism).
2. To build sleeping quarters (search for security).
3. To look for the quickest way to get where someone has just told them to go in no uncertain terms.

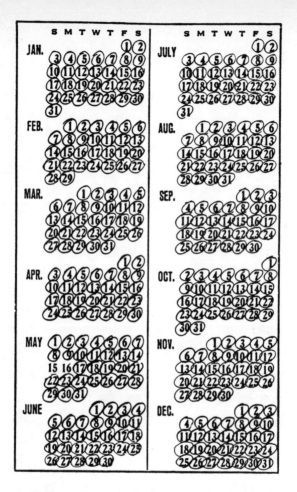

When is the time for your dog to have his vacation? In the summer? (It may be too hot for him.) In the winter? (It may be too cold.) During the spring or fall? (These seasons may be neither warm nor cool enough.) Fortunately, the problem is not as complicated as it sounds. Circles around dates show exactly when, in the dog's opinion, is the right time for vacationing.

76

Summary

1. **DO** take the dog with you on vacations. Remember, he, too, needs the rest.

2. **DON'T** make him feel unwanted. Let him have the back-seat of the car, if possible. If you have no backseat, get another car.

3. **DO** choose your vacation spots with him in mind.

4. **DON'T** consider taking your dog to faraway places. You just may get inspired to leave him there.

CHAPTER 6

Feeding the Neurotic Dog

Dog owners often complain that their dogs eat like pigs. Not so. Dogs do not eat like pigs, or even like horses. They eat like dogs.

The speed with which a dog can make food disappear has long been considered a true scientific curiosity. What enables him to do so is his capacity to swallow food whole. There has been some speculation as to why dogs go without chewing; the answer is, of course, that chewing takes up valuable time.

Dogs eat because of insecurity. Experience tells them we might eat what belongs to them before they get a chance, a situation that comes up especially when food is put on the dining table.

It is perfectly all right to keep the dog's dish in the kitchen for easy access. Next to the bedroom, the dog's favorite room is the kitchen. As a matter of fact, in the dog's mind, your home probably looks like this:

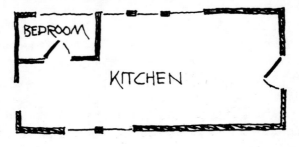

And here's his notion of a kitchen:

Contrary to popular belief, the dog is not an omnivorous animal. He may accept an occasional egg, tomato, or radish garnish, but basically he is carnivorous.

That's because dog's ancestors stem from the wolf family (*Canis lupus*). His instinct tells him to head straight for beef, veal, lamb, pâté de foie gras, or whatever meat is included on the menu at the time.

Whatever dog lacks in table manners, he makes up in showmanship to get attention and the ultimate reward for his antics, namely, to be invited to join the others at the table.

Act 1: He appears slowly behind the table, his eyes glistening, nostrils quivering, and mouth salivating.

Act 2: He performs for his audience, displaying his remarkable athletic skills.

Act 3: He takes his seat.

DOG BISCUITS

WATER

Man's concept of dog's meal shows lack of understanding of basic canine needs.

ENTREES

Calf's Liver Steak Sauté, Smothered Onions, Mashed Potatoes ....
Filet of Veal Goulash à la Minute en Casserole, Rice ....
Calf's Sweetbreads Broiled, Potatoes; Bouquetière ....
Hamburger Steak, Smothered Onions, Mashed Potatoes ....
Capon Cutlets, Creamed Mushrooms, Rissolé Potato ....
*Home Made Bratwurst, Sauerkraut, Mashed Potatoes ....
(2) Broiled Lamb Chops ....
Fresh Vegetable Dinner with Fried Egg ....
Huhn im Topf, (Boiled Chicken in Pot), Gemüse, Nudeln, Klösschen
Chicken Fricassée with Rice; White Meat Only ....
Fried Chicken à la Viennoise, Lettuce and Tomato, Rissolé Potato ....
*Sauerbraten und Kartoffel Klösse ....
*Boiled Plate of Beef with Horseradish Sauce, Bouillon Potatoes ....
Jumbo Squab on Winekraut en Bordure or Jardinière ....
Fresh Chicken Livers Sauté with Apple Rings, Onions, Mashed Potatoes
(2) Pork Chops Broiled ....
Corned Pig's Knuckles, Sauerkraut, Mashed Potatoes ....:...........

FISH AND SEAFOOD

Filet of Sea Bass Sauté with Seedless Grapes, Boiled Potatoes
Boiled or Broiled Kennebec Salmon, Cucumber Salad .....
Broiled Pompano Maitre d'Hotel, Creamed Potatoes .....
Lobster Curried with Rice or à la Newburg, Chafing Dish
Broiled Swordfish, Potatoes; Jardinière ....
Halibut Steak, Broiled, Parsley Potatoes ....
Frog's Legs Fried or Sauté Meunière, Mixed Salad ....
Fried Long Island Scallops, Tartar Sauce ....
Whole Imported English Sole Sauté Meunière, Mixed Salad
Crabflakes Creamed, Sherry Sauce, Glazed ....
Fried Filet of Sole, Tartar Sauce, Potato Salad ....
State of Maine Lobster, Broiled ....

CHEESE	FRUITS, COMPOTES
Imported Roquefort	Imported Bar-le-Duc ....
Welsh Rarebit	Baked Apple ....
Old Cheddar with Sherry .	Melon in Season ....
Camembert	Apple Sauce ....
Liederkranz	Half Grapefruit ....
Philadelphia Cream Cheese ..	Importierte Preiselbeeren ....
Pot Cheese	Fruit Cocktail ....
Blue Cheese, Imported Type	Sliced Fruit in Season with Cream
Canadian Okra	Berries in Season with Cream ....
Imported Swiss Gruyere	Compote of Fruit ....

Dog's concept of menu clearly shows major differences of opinion as to his dietary requirements.

83

You may wish to put your dog on a diet. A dog with a double chin makes a poor impression, except if he is a bulldog. There are reducing plans now available to fit dogs of every size and shape: large, small, round, triangular, and quadrangular.

It is for you to decide whether or not your dog is over-eating, as he will always opine he is just the right height and width. As a rule, when your dog is no longer able to cross the room and has a tendency to roll over, it is time to cut down his food intake. Try keeping him away from anything edible for several hours.

Other warning signs: your dog no longer fits into the bathtub; his belly reaches the floor; the bed collapses under his weight; he cannot make it through the front door; you can no longer tell the difference between his front and back end; your child keeps confusing the dog with his beachball.

Another way to make your dog lose weight is putting him on a vigorous exercise program. Let him jump in your lap instead of picking him up. Increase the distance between the bed and his dish. Have him approach you, instead of the other way around. Don't let him sit and watch television all the time.

Dog dish may please you but not necessarily your dog. Consider these special feeding devices to help him eat more in less time:

Food passing through feeder chute is chopped into smaller particles, sliced and diced for easy consumption. Spout can be adjusted to satisfy dog's particular needs.

Nosebag enables dog to eat in any position: standing, walking, going about his business. Especially popular with dogs who like to eat on the move.

Summary

1. **DO** feed your dog regularly, say, on the hour.

2. **DON'T** give him food fit for a dog. Remember, man invented dog food, not dogs. They were not even consulted.

3. **DO** invite him to join you at the table. Let him know what's yours is his; what's his is his.

4. **DON'T** be misled by the size of your dog in relation to the amount he eats. You may be larger than your dog, but you don't work as hard. He needs those calories.

CHAPTER 7

The Neurotic Dog vs. Baby

One of the most traumatic experiences in a dog's life is the arrival of a baby in the family. This addition to the household completely upsets the dog's well-established routine and diverts attention from his presence, in spite of the fact that the human infant is obviously both physically and intellectually inferior to the dog. (More about this later.) Be that as it may, all babies strike a dog as a breed in desperate need of improvement; it is doubtful that the species could pass even the most rudimentary requirements of the American Kennel Association.

Yet his owner seems to hold the new arrival in as much, if not greater, esteem as the incumbent now at the premises. The baby is fed not twice, but five or six times a day. His screaming, loud enough to send the resident canine to

hide in a closet, makes the owner come running. His mischief is greeted with a silly grin and such responses, as "Isn't he a dear?" or "He's so full of life, isn't he now?"

He is not housebroken and shows little interest in learning, but this, too, is blithely overlooked. He is held, cuddled, and spoken to in soothing tones. When he hollers at night (which is often), he is not put out the back door as was the custom before he came; rather, he is rocked to sleep. His cries are explained away as lung exercise, his pulling his owner's ears as zest for life, his dribbling at the mouth as a sign of healthy appetite.

It soon becomes apparent to a dog that what's taking place shouldn't happen to a dog. Everything tells him that . . .

Someone else is getting all the attention!

Explained below is dog's emotional dilemma with the arrival of new baby. Dog (D) tries to get attention of Mother (M) by following established strategy; i.e., walking up to her. Abruptly cut off by Baby (B), and trying to avoid open confrontation, dog walks around Baby. But Baby again blocks his way. (See dotted lines.) Mother now approaches Baby, ignores Dog.

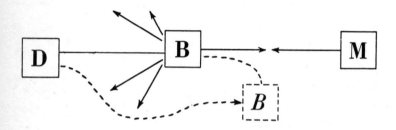

Mother must now learn to deal with sibling rivalry in the family. She must understand how the dog feels deep down—why he is trying to dispose of the new occupant by pulling him out the door while no one is watching.

There are ways to establish peace in the family.

1. Let the dog know beforehand that he is going to have a little brother or sister whose needs will not interfere with his.

2. Don't fuss over the baby in view of the dog.

3. Never buy a more expensive toy for the baby than for the dog at Christmas.

4. Tell baby it isn't nice to bite a dog.

Slow physical development of baby only proves to dog what he suspected all along: he is superior in every way. As the months go by, the physical differences between the animal and the human become increasingly obvious, leaving no doubt about whose development is more rapid.

TWO MONTHS.   SIX MONTHS.

TWELVE MONTHS.

Quick comparisons also show that the dog is superior to the infant in every way. Baby develops slowly, has difficulties in learning, speaks in tongues, and depends on the good graces of his elders. In time, dog leaves human infant far behind in intellectual achievement, capacity to use logic, word comprehension, and just plain common sense.

BABY	DOG
Four Weeks He breathes with regularity. He can cry and open his eyes wide. He can turn his head.	**Four Weeks** He breathes with regularity. He can cry and open his eyes wide. He can turn his head.
Sixteen Weeks He can turn over to his back and try sitting up. His eyes follow moving object, and he may even reach out for it. But he cannot grasp it, for all his ten fingers.	**Sixteen Weeks** The puppy can walk steadily across the room, sit, lie down, and stand up. He can follow a moving object with his eyes and, if it is food, grasp it.
Twenty-eight Weeks The baby can sit up, but he still topples over. He can reach for desired object and bring it to his mouth. He can even grab his feet and put them in his mouth as he lies on his back.	**Twenty-eight Weeks** At this age, a puppy can do many things. He can get under blankets. He can chew up books, shoes, and carpets. He is smart enough not to waste his time sucking his feet.
One Year The baby creeps about freely on hands and knees. He is beginning to discover the world at his own pace: slowly.	**One Year** The dog can now run so fast that his master can no longer catch him. He knows all he needs to know.
Two Years The baby finally understands part of what is being said. He is even able to utter a few words, even if they do not make sense. Lost for words, he giggles.	**Two Years** The dog understands everything that is said. He even understands that at times it is wiser to pretend he doesn't understand and keep his nozzle shut.

It doesn't take the dog long to learn that he must now fight for his rights. His methods will vary, depending on his natural resourcefulness and his ability to make others feel guilty for ignoring his presence.

Attention can be captured by moving in close, putting head lovingly on owner's shoulders.

Howling in harmony with baby will make others take notice, even if a dog is less than musically inclined.

Sharing meals serves to remind all that our basic needs
are very much alike.

Baby's first steps can easily be duplicated to impress
one's impressionable parents.

The reader may surmise from this chapter that a baby and a dog are always at odds. Nothing could be further from the truth. In no time at all, the two will learn from one another and act in unison. This can be a source of much pleasure to both the baby and the dog, if not the owner.

For example, there is the matter of toys. As far as the dog is concerned, his human friend's playthings are as good as his own. Covered with nontoxic paint, they taste just fine.

Most dogs will submit cheerfully to playing with human infants. They will wrestle with the little one, tearing his pants to pieces to the joy of both. They will play hide-and-seek both in the home and away from it, to be discovered only by the police and the fire department hours later. They will learn to share things, as should be expected of offspring of the same family; dog will participate at baby's meals, and vice versa.

Soon, the parents will come to think of the dog as just another one of their children. This will not come as a surprise to the dog, since that is exactly what he had in mind all along.

Summary

1. **DON'T** make your dog feel he is second to the baby, especially if he was there first.

2. **DO** consider that just because dog condescends to playing with the human infant, it does not mean he considers the baby an intellectual equal. In his opinion, at least, his is a better-developed brain and is able to solve more complex problems.

3. **DON'T** hold it against your dog if he withdraws for a few days after baby's arrival. He needs time to sort things out and think of ways to cope with the intrusion.

4. **DO** let your dog know as soon as he is old enough to understand that in spite of what he thinks, you are *not* his natural parent.

CHAPTER 8

The Neurotic Dog and Your Cat

Next to the human infant, dog's greatest natural enemy is *Felis domesticus*, also known as pussycat. The ubiquitous presence of this animal calls for major readjustments not only in the dog's lifestyle, but in his thinking as well.

These two species obviously were put on earth for entirely different reasons. Cats are supposed to catch mice. Dogs go after bigger and more formidable prey, such as other dogs. Wagging the tail is a canine characteristic; at most, cats only twitch their tails, and then only to shoo off flies or to let the owner know he is boring them. With such diverse personalities, it's no wonder that the two animals often fail to come to an agreement, formal or informal.

And that isn't all. As a practical matter, both cats and dogs are after exactly the same thing: room and board. Clearly, there is a conflict of interests between the two.

It seems to the dog that cats succeed in making a favorable impression with hardly an effort; their mere presence is all that is required. Dog must work harder to earn his keep. More likely than not, his personal worth is judged by his education, past accomplishments, and willingness to please all two-footed creatures in the household.

Good Dog
He is a fine watchdog.
He is a great retriever.
He rolls over on command.
He can walk on his hind legs.

Good Cat
He is cute.

As a rule, it is the dog who gets blamed for every accident in the home: spilled milk, chewed-up pillows, empty refrigerators, and scratch marks on the baby's face. This is because dogs tend to appear guiltier than cats. A sharp rebuke promptly sends a dog's tail between his legs and turns his face from gladsome to gloomy. These are sure signs of a troubled conscience. Cats have no such compunctions. Nature gave them a face that is expressionless. Contrary to popular belief, a cat who just swallowed a canary looks no different from one who did not.

Then, too, cats have the perfect alibi; they are never at the scene of the crime. No dog can ever hope to disappear as fast and as completely as a cat.

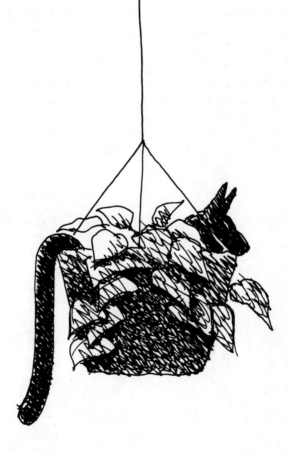

Able to change shape at will, cats have a wide choice of hiding places in case of emergency. They greatly respect privacy—their own.

It is said that a cat always lands on his feet when dropped. This is true. Through a series of remarkable aerial maneuvers, cats are able to keep their balance.

Less accomplished is dog's performance. He may try to land on all fours, but with mixed results. The force of gravity almost always wins out; his head being the heaviest part of his body, it makes contact with the ground first.

Nothing can block the path of the cat trying to get from one point to another in a hurry, least of all a dog.

Ability to jump high into the air using vertical take-off gives the cat an important advantage. Cat can aspire to reach heights far out of dog's reach, no matter how hard the latter tries to jump. Good intentions do not make up for being a born klutz.

Dog musing about his feline roommate:
I WISH HE WOULD BE SAT ON ... FALL OUT OF A
TREE ... GET PICKED UP BY A BIRD OF PREY ...
BE TAKEN FOR A WALK ON A LEASH ... BE
CHOSEN TO BECOME THE WORLD'S FIRST
TRAINED CAT ... BE MISTAKEN FOR A DOG BY A
DOGCATCHER ... LOSE HIS WAY HOME ... BE
GIVEN A BATH ... BE SHOT TO THE MOON ...

107

Cats Can Be Such a Pain in the Neck!

Summary

1. **DO** formally introduce your cat to your dog.

2. **DON'T** expect your cat to obey commands. As any cat owner knows, this is beneath feline dignity.

3. **DO** learn to distinguish between a purr and a growl. Cats purr when they feel good. Dogs growl when they do not.

4. **DON'T** expect your dog to smile at your cat or vice-versa.

5. **DO** separate the two by hand if there is no other way to end the argument.

6. **DON'T** expect your cat to smile at your dog.

CHAPTER 9

How to Play with a Neurotic Dog

It is not true that all your neurotic dog has on his mind is food and shelter. His interests are much wider than that, his horizon broader. Between naps and mealtimes he may also want to play. This is a healthy sign, if not for you, then for your dog. Most play involves activity—a step in the right direction.

It is important that in both body and spirit you are there for your dog whenever he feels like playing. The mood may strike him any time during the day or night. Dogs do not like to play alone. They prefer having company and letting someone else do the work.

If you see your dog is getting tired—or, more likely, getting bored—stop pushing him. He probably needs a rest.

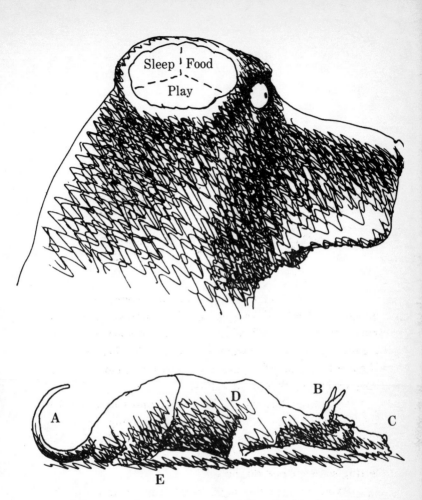

Signs of incipient activity can be observed while dog lies in repose. They are: (A) tail twitching, (B) ears pricking, (C) nostrils flaring, (D) chest heaving, and (E) legs shaking. This dog is about to rouse from his stupor.

111

Horses rarely, if ever, engage in horseplay, but dogs do. Dog's capacity for having a good time shows up at an early age. Even as a puppy, dog enjoys roughhousing with his master and taking small bites out of his toes. As he grows bigger, so does the size of his bites.

ONE MONTH.

FIVE MONTHS.

EIGHT MONTHS.

ONE YEAR.

Dogs are all for vigorous exercise. They find the idea worth pursuing. They know that physical activity helps you, the owner and provider of all good things, lose weight, develop coordination, and most important, improve your outlook on life, which hasn't been so good lately.

For all the above reasons, dog will happily participate in your exertions, sharing your good spirit in every way. Both your physical and mental health are very much on his mind; he wants to keep you well. Shown here are dogs and their owners working out *together* in perfect harmony, just as nature intended.

Bicycle rides improve your cardiovascular capacity, develop endurance, lower cholesterol.

Jogging provides important aerobic benefits, improves
muscle tone, gets you home faster.

Touching the ground with your hands is one of the best stretching exercises. It is also one of the easiest to master—at least it is for the dog.

Summary

1. **DO** work out with your dog. It's good for *you*.

2. **DON'T** ask him to play with you only at your convenience. Keep his schedule in mind, too.

3. **DO** stop playing when he falls asleep.

4. **DON'T** try to win every time. It's bad for his ego.

5. **DO** pretend you are enjoying his company.

CHAPTER 10

Analyzing the Neurotic Dog at Home

Psychoanalysis can be expensive, especially if both dog and master must undergo treatment. Fortunately, the cost now can be reduced. Today there are do-it-yourself methods for analyzing your dog right where you live. All you need are a soft couch on which the dog can stretch himself out, a hard chair for you to sit on, and a box of facial tissues to wipe away your tears as you learn more about your subject's early childhood experiences.

Dogs make cooperative patients; they may actually enjoy the experience. In no time at all they sink into a state of semiconsciousness, also known as sleep.

Analysis is, of course, a slow, tedious process, and success should not be expected overnight. The length of treatment may vary anywhere from ten to twenty years, depending on your dog's lifespan.

Position of your dog on the couch will reveal much about his inner life. Relaxed, easy-going type usually sits comfortably at the end of the couch.

Hiding under cushions is a sign of insecurity and desire for privacy. This patient needs special attention, definitely special upholstery.

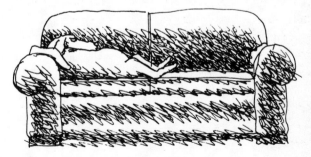

And finally, a dog tired of living.

A quiet, darkened room, devoid of distraction, creates the ideal environment for analysis to proceed.

CANINE PERSONALITY QUIZ

Score plus five for each affirmative answer to questions one, two, three, and seven. Score minus five for each affirmative answer to questions four, five, six, and eight. If you have a plus answer, your dog is basically an introvert; if you have a minus answer, your dog is basically an extrovert.

You are neither an introvert nor an extrovert if you failed to follow the instructions above. You're just not paying any attention.

	Yes	No
1. Does your dog particularly enjoy watching soap operas on television?	( )	( )
2. Does he wag his tail at the sight of burglars breaking into the house?	( )	( )
3. Does he join community singing and mouth the words?	( )	( )
4. Does he take long walks alone?	( )	( )
5. Does he frown when you talk to him?	( )	( )
6. Does he sniff at his food suspiciously before taking the first bite?	( )	( )
7. Does he spend much of his time chasing imaginary flies?	( )	( )
8. Does he start his day with a shot of whiskey?	( )	( )

Explanation:

1. If your dog likes to watch soap operas, he is looking for an escape. He is an introvert.

2. Welcoming visitors to your home shows a friendly disposition. He is an extrovert.

3. Singing in a group indicates a desire to belong. He is an extrovert.

4. Only thinkers go on solitary walks. Your dog is either a thinker or he is trying to save the cost of transportation. Either way, he is an introvert.

5. He is skeptical about what you're telling him, probably rightly so. He is an introvert.

6. Sniffing at food to see if it is poisoned is a sign of paranoia. He is an introvert.

7. Chasing flies, especially imaginary ones, makes no sense, but it lends purpose to life. He is an extrovert.

8. Compulsive alcoholics drink first thing in the morning. He is none too pleased with the way things are going. He is an introvert.

The shape of a dog's skull tells much about his brain (if he has one, that is). The most commonly known are egghead, pumpkinhead, squarehead, and the inverted-pyramid head. Known for his small-sized brain is the pinhead.

Of the greatest significance, according to canine phrenologists, are the bumps on a dog's head and what they represent. Round knob (1) at the end of the nasal bone structure functions as an olfactory organ and is helpful to the dog looking for food, his master, or another dog. Domelike protuberance near the top (2) is considered by many a sign of intelligence, though this is mere speculation. It is here that information is stored and processed, after entering by way of nose, eyes (3), and ears (4). Nature has given many dogs rather large lobes to protect them from hearing what they would just as soon not. Slight rise on the back of dog's head (5) is only a so-called temporary bump visible after a fight or landing top end.

126

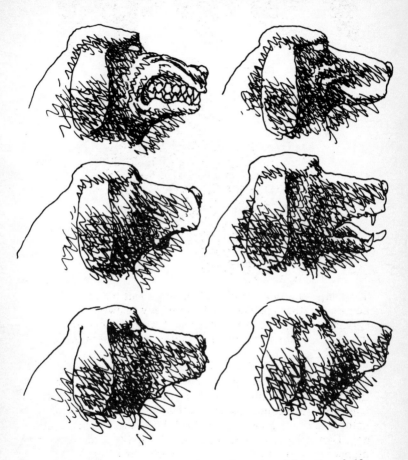

The sleeping dog's expressions give away his natural, if hidden, opinions of the world around him, such as hostility, envy, greed, and general disgust.

The *Obstacle Course* tests animal intelligence as well as determination. Dogs rank high on both counts. Taking the shortest route to where they want to go, and not easily discouraged by everyday, ordinary obstacles, dogs manage to reach their goal in short order.

129

The *Alertness Test* is a simple procedure and is easy to execute in your home. Just call your dog by his given name (or names that just happen to occur to you at the moment) and watch his reactions, if any.

Average dog will react in less than five minutes, depending on the pitch and strength of your voice. Polite by nature, he will listen to what it is you want to tell him before going back to sleep.

Exceptionally alert dog will probably open his eyes sooner and keep them that way a little longer. He may even look at you and give you a fleeting if somewhat crooked smile.

Relaxed dog knows you're just trying to put him to the test. Since he will keep his eyes shut, there is no sure way of checking his reaction to your voice, or even what he is thinking.

The *Sociability Test* helps you to measure your dog's interest in his fellow dogs. Healthy, well-adjusted dogs will greet one another, exchange routine information, and then be on their way to strike up a new and perhaps more promising acquaintance.

Now . . . At Last . . .
You Understand Your Dog

Summary

1. **DO** psychoanalyze your dog. It will help him to face himself and, more important, face you.

2. **DON'T** waste your money on professional fees for your dog's analysis. You will need that money to pay for your own treatments.

3. **DO** hide your notes from your dog.

4. **DON'T** hurry with the analysis. Remember: your dog likes to lie on the couch.

5. **DO** keep your dog, even though results of analysis tell you otherwise.

CHAPTER 11

Can the Neurotic Dog Be Cured?

No.

THE END